The Anthology oj

THE ANTHOLOGY *of* TOMORROW

Flapjack Press
www.flapjackpress.co.uk

Exploring the synergy between performance and the page

Published in 2019 by Flapjack Press
Salford, Gtr Manchester
www.flapjackpress.co.uk

ISBN 978-1-9996707-6-9-5

Cover design by Brink
www.paulneads.co.uk

Printed by Imprint Digital
Upton Pyne, Exeter, Devon
imprintdigital.com

**City of
Literature**

*With thanks to everyone who has helped
and supported Flapjack Press over the years,
and to its occasionally unstable stable of poets
who, in honouring the ancient rites of publishing,
will often confuse 'yesterday' and 'tomorrow'
when it comes to deadlines.*

Contents

Foreword

Flapjack Press has been going for a good few years now and this anthology of poems is probably long overdue. With a tenet of publishing performance poetry, especially that from the North-West, its profile has increased year on year, and in 2018 Flapjack was shortlisted for the Northern Publisher of the Year at the Northern Soul Awards. Whilst not winning (though garnering the congratulatory slap on the back of a Special Mention), it was due recognition for all the poets published.

And so, it was deemed rather a good time to get everyone together in one collection, both a showcase and a sampler, primarily of new and specially commissioned work.

After a bit of head-scratching, a theme was decided upon: 'Tomorrow'. Something forward-thinking, something enlightening, something filled with hope (and from a suggestion by one of the poets you will find within these pages, Henry Normal). But at the back of my mind I was always wary of setting a theme. I recall, back in the day when I edited an old poetry magazine, that one month I received thirty poems about an orange sent from a workshop group in the USA. It would certainly have filled the pages and saved a bit of time on advertising for submissions, but probably have led to the cancellation of quite a few subscriptions (apart from those from the Rutaceae family and their friends).

Such concerns have definitely proven to be unfounded. Herein, you will find stimulating and engaging poetry worth your investment of time (plus cover price). I hope that you find them as interesting and eclectic as our stable, and any citrus fruit involved is worthy of its place.

Welcome to *The Anthology of Tomorrow*.

Paul Neads
Editor

THE ANTHOLOGY *of* TOMORROW

DOMINIC BERRY

"Really very inspiring."
Benjamin Zephaniah, poet

Dominic is a Manchester-based performance poet, whose work has taken him across Europe, and tours of the USA, Canada, Argentina, India, Australia and New Zealand.

He has been Glastonbury Festival's poet-in-residence and his awards include winning Manchester Literature Festival's Superheroes of Slam, New York's Nuyorican Poetry Café Slam, and he was publicly voted Saboteur Awards' Best Spoken Word Performer.

Titles: *Tomorrow, I Will Go Dancing,*
Wizard & *No Tigers.*

For children (as Dommy B): *The Stories of… Spark, the Goblin Wizard, When Trolls Try to Eat Your Goldfish, The Dragon Who Hates Poetry* & *Aaaaaaaaaaaaagh! Dinosaurs!*

Tomorrow, I Will Go Dancing

Today, I'm eating margarine straight from the tub
and I feel so guilty however hard I scrub.
My wrist's unbandaged, I'm trying not to rub,
but I've so many sores that need lancing.
Tomorrow, I will go dancing.

My fingernails are rusty. Head's full of ills.
Chest hot and tender as stomach spills.
But tomorrow, I'm going to get these little pills.
See, everything about me needs enhancing.
Tomorrow, I will go dancing.

Tomorrow, you'll go dancing in your glitter tat.
Absinthe! Vodka! You never get fat.
Laughing. Smiling. All that goes with that.
Today, I feel anxieties advancing.
Tomorrow, I will go dancing.

Hear my father's voice, warped and splintered today.
He says, *"Misery will find you, boy. You'll never get away."*
My dick feels like a beehive on a warm summer's day
when I see pretty things all preening and prancing.
Tomorrow, I will go dancing.

Everyone there's friendly. Falling into song.
I want to be loved. I've been lonely for so long.
Tomorrow is a vessel, sail way from all this wrong
where bitches say I'm ugly and can't sing.
Tomorrow, I will go dancing.

Today, I feel your laughter and it's gnawing in my head,
it is biting out the blisters where you burned until I bled,
if I panic... 'til I can't breathe, feel I'd be better dead,
well, I tell myself that risk is worth chancing.
Tomorrow, I will go dancing.

I want to join the happy crowds, glorious and glad.
I want to like pop music. Never feel bad.
My therapist's implying that I choose to be this sad.
I tell her, *"You know nothing... but if you're asking..."*

I think she's asking?

She's asking.

"Tomorrow, I will go dancing."

You. Me. A man who we believe to be about our age. He wears a t-shirt, shorts, no shoes, sits silently on a small, clean scrap of corrugated cardboard in a derelict shop's doorway. Pedestrians pass his static hand. By his side, two barefoot toddlers play with plastic trucks.

Red light. Two boys race into traffic. The smaller leaps onto the taller's shoulders and four fast hands are suddenly juggling six bright white skittles.

Car occupants silently sit, heads and hands full of steering wheel and gear stick. Feet tense on accelerators. A red light might temporarily hold their bodies here, but eyes already reflect their next destination.

The smaller boy bounces down and asks at each car for money, but these drivers seem more like shadows than people, only affected by the changing light.

We are struggling to connect to this city's WiFi. On my palm I've made a biro map to replace our sat-nav, but in this heat the sweaty city streets are smeared. We try to look like we know where we are and where we are going.

Towering Spoken Word

The spirit of Leonard Cohen has spoken to me and revealed he believes all my poetry is awful.

At first, I did feel disappointed by the prosaic approach of this critique. Had Cohen made the effort to assess my work whilst actually alive, I believe his damnation would have surely included some oblique reference to spiderwebs or oranges to sweeten the blow. I have spent a lifetime defending *Death of a Ladies' Man* for this.

However, I remember when the spirit of Marvin Gaye spoke to Terence Trent D'Arby and gave him the song 'To Know Someone Deeply is to Know Someone Softly', making him believe he was good enough to make that song a hit. Marvin Gaye's ghost literally killed Terence Trent D'Arby's career with praise. Cohen's posthumous assassination of mine is in fact his final act of mercy and wisdom; this is a blessing through which my past mistakes will now be wiped aside, allowing my true genius to finally begin.

STEPH PIKE

"That one person at the party you can have a real conversation with."
Helen Mort, Derbyshire Poet Laureate

A feminist socialist activist, Steph performs regularly across the country, including at many left-wing and feminist demos and rallies.

She organises guerrilla poetry protests, is a committee member of Manchester People's Assembly (part of the national movement against cuts and austerity), and is passionate about the personal and political transformative power of poetry.

Title: *Pétroleuse.*

Neon

fireflies, will o' the wisp
ghosts on your retina
night snaps out our words

we talk salty back pocket semaphore
code knocked out on
anonymous doors we inhabit

clubs, back alley, underground
pumping hearts searching
for a way back

to the stars, we sip cocktails
delicate as humming birds, inhale
from cistern tops and strangers' keys

our blood floods with music
we dance sublime until
so hot, so wanting

we pull each other into cubicles
agile as otters, in this small space
we make the cracked walls noble

mouths, liquid fingers
unclothing molten cores
the sweat-swilled floor shakes

as dawn breaks, the earth can barely contain us
we are too volatile
we scatter like mercury

Early Snow Fall

a cold snap
a sudden drop
the clouds are shivery, unsettled
crystal breath streams
persistent as grief
the flakes are thick and slow
tonight they do not want to land
they whisper against each other
so many of us have fallen
voices lost in the blizzard
white noise, amnesia, cataract

tomorrow
nothing will be the same
the landscape ice-burned
all features gone
the world a silent monochrome
our sins died in the wool
on Christmas morning
the body of a young woman
is found under a layer of snow

PETE RAMSKILL

"Why are you so angry?"
Audience member at the BBC

Pete is a Southport-born poet, artist, designer and sculptor, who appeared on BBC 3's *Whine Gums* poetry series.

He used to perform regularly on Terry Christian's Radio Derby show and has performed at the Edinburgh Festival for BBC Radio 4.

Title: *Selected moments of machine life.*

Futures

I have carried the weight of the future
On one shoulder
I have lowered the future
With purple bands
Slipping through my hands
Into the ground
Then tossed roses into the darkness

The only future
We will all know

And if
As I search for the humanist equivalent
Of 'heaven forbid'
When my turn comes
There is one of the many gods on offer
Stood waiting
Finger wagging
And pointing at the shit-pit
I will have my say

So you are hard boiled vindictive
Uncaring
Callous
And if that was the best case you could put
Down there on our speck of dust
Then it was feeble
Unconvincing
Confused
And presented by charlatans

The blind leading the stupid

Voices

In a quiet moment of uncertainty
a voice said
know yourself
and was followed by silence

Then, another voice
less familiar
assured yet unconcerned said
all that is not known
is in doubt
causing a reflection and a chill

Closed eyes confirmed the darkness
and in the shadows of darkness
a third voice
rose slowly
and sang a soothing song
in sensual tones affirming
there is only doubt

Tomorrow Becomes...

In all probability the sun will rise
Just like it did today
So it's a good thing the winning ticket was bought
The future secured
Everything sorted
Everything in its place
The world put to rights
Hopes and dreams realised
Items to be actioned and ticked-off

Only a few things slipping by
To be added to the fluff in the seams of pockets
The irritating wish that lingers
To be added to the list
Of things to do when conditions allow
When the situation seems right
Not now
Another list of excuses to be drawn up
After all
Today just becomes yesterday's tomorrow

ROSIE GARLAND

"A national treasure."
Dead Good Poets Society

Recently named "literary hero" by *The Skinny*, Rosie is an award-winning poet, novelist and singer with post-punk band The March Violets.

With a passion for language nurtured by libraries, she started out in spoken word, garnering praise from Apples and Snakes as "one of the country's finest performance poets".

Her debut novel, *The Palace of Curiosities* [HarperCollins, 2013], was nominated for both The Desmond Elliott and the Polari First Book Prize and won Book of the Year in the Co-op Respect Awards 2013. Her second novel, *Vixen* [Borough Press, 2014], was a Green Carnation Prize nominee. Her third, *The Night Brother*, was published in 2017.

Titles: *Things I Did While I Was Dead*
& *As in Judy*.

When You Grow Up

At night, she leaps and does not land. Spreads her arms and soars
above the fenced and neatly weeded garden. Her dreams
are practice sessions where she lifts cars, sees through walls, fights

dragons. She is a pirate captain, a queen, a horse. She is neither girl
nor boy: the distinctions are irrelevant when her small body
    encompasses
male and female; human, beast. A turbulent child figure-heading

the prow of her beaked ship, she buckles on armour, rescues
princesses from charming princes and spinning wheels.
She is fearless of the shapes beneath the bed. Too soon

she hears the summons: *Breakfast! Now!*
Blinks this world into focus. Hushes battle cries,
sheathes her sword between the pages of her book.

Every bedtime her mother tucks in
the sheet of husband, marriage, children: tucks it in tight.

You Will Find Yourself

Title after David Byrne, 'Once in a lifetime'.

When it happens
birds will suddenly appear every time you are near
stars will fall down from the sky every time you walk by
you will have four wishes
the right change
there will always be a seat
the moon will say *I thought you'd never ask*
and hand itself to you on a stick

Daily Mail readers will hurl away their newspapers
shouting *we won't be fed this bullshit*
in a nationwide chorus of disgust
Politicians will admit they're greedy, self-serving
and lie through their teeth
Abusers will not die peacefully in their sleep

God will announce she was only joking
has been widely misquoted
would rather spend her time designing star-nosed moles
and playing with all her other universes

You will write that opera, that play, that poem
take up pottery or crochet or hang gliding
you will run for buses, smile on buses, sing on buses
tap dance down the canned goods aisle of Aldi
ears ringing with tickertape applause
as shoppers unpop their earplugs and cheer

The bullies will say sorry
you'll stop reading the glossy magazines
that police your failures
lover number three will return that little piece of your heart

Your trousers will have pockets in which you can fit your fists
enough money for escaping
and a stack of detailed plans for the revolution

You will stop searching the screen for your future
put your phone on silent
slide it in your bag
take your hand away from its smooth operator lies

All the times you said *yes* and didn't want to will roar *no*
the times you said *no* but didn't want to will roar *yes*
bruises will unpeel their yellow foliage
and your dreams will sprout roses, fat and heavy with perfume

You will stop swallowing the bitter meat of hatred
dished up as honesty
feed yourself kindness
from recipes filled with delicious friendship

Words you wrote in anger will unravel, lift from the page
melt into ink and swim back into the pen
nib poised, ready to start again

You will not have a thigh gap
nor lose one inch of belly fat a day
nor get a six-pack in 4 weeks
nor spritz up your life with a new sofa, kitchen, or life laundry
You will be enough

Nights will wrap their arms around you
evenings will have skies of lucky red delight
and you'll run into the open arms of Monday mornings
taste the spice of sunrise
and spread its salsa on days that brim generous

You will unfuck your life

There will be no hell, nor heaven
angels will hold off sounding final trumpets
the rapture will stay unraptured
mountains will pause their transformation into valleys
the lake of fire will keep its cool
the mouth of hell will button its lip

as you unbuckle the rack of punishment and reward
walk away from happy-ever-after glittery illusion
unlock doors
carry yourself across their thresholds
and get out of jail free

You will be surprised at how small it is
how such a little thing could look so big
do so much damage

You will not forgive
You will not forget
but you will find a place for the memories to sleep

You will stand on every pavement crack
and bears will say they never liked being a metaphor
You will breathe out
clear your lungs of anxious tar

You will slow down
sit on park benches and look up
read the swirl of birds, clouds, light
aeroplane trails spelling today's adventure
the first letter of your name
the first line of your novel

You will take up space

You will love who you want to love
you will tell them how much you love them, often
and believe them when they reply

Your internal critic will throw in the towel, fall silent
words losing their edge of slaughter
and the velvet peace inside your head will unroll carpets
draw back curtains to reveal a view that is clear and unbroken

You will not have your time again
but each tomorrow is a chance
to walk down a different street
take a different fork in the road
or the same fork
and there, in the last place you thought to look –

you will love yourself
you will forgive yourself

DERMOT GLENNON

"Funny, hard and relatable."
Lauren Bolger, Paradox

Dr Dermot Glennon is a Silver Stake poetry slam-winning performer and a prize-winning author of short stories in multiple genres.

An inveterate seeker (and cause) of scandal, he is also possibly one of the greatest poets and philosophers of the last two centuries by virtue of this being totally subjective and non-specific.

Title: *Anthems and Album Tracks.*

You Will Rise

One day in righteous passion
of a kind that burns forests
you will stand on the rock
and hold forth
and deliver

Deliver the words of an aeon
for an age
you will talk the hind legs off a donkey
you will save the planet on which it stands
on its two front legs

With its head in its hands
you will save the world of a donkey
you will save its world with your words
you will bore the arse off a donkey
its world saved

Its hind legs both gone
its arse bored off
you love the planet
you love all its creatures
you have something against that donkey

And
you won't look after yourself
talk to Ronnie Real here
don't be some lone crusader
don't crusade
it does you nothing

It does you no good
it wears you down
it's not immoral to look after yourself
it's kind of moral
to take care of yourself

You will not get the recognition you feel you deserve
you're not Wyld Stallyns
you can't do forever
what you do today
they'll drag you away

The world waits
it waits for you to find
step outside
don't live in your own head
grab entirety by its celestial spheres

and squeeze
until it capitulates and agrees
Do it
not often
and you will rise

Final Instructions

I used to want a large stone
at my head

inscribed with big letters
NOT RESTING JUST DEAD

Now I want a tiny one
on the ground instead

such that to read the writing
you have to bow your head

No eulogy do I ask for
just the basic facts

I'm neither dead nor resting
I'm behind you with an axe

DAVE MORGAN

"The flame of Beat poetry still flickers brightly."
Greg Freeman, writer & reviewer

Dave is a writer, educationalist and community arts organiser in the North-West of England.

In 2004, he co-founded the performance poetry organisation Write Out Loud with Julian Jordon, and more recently has been a co-curator of the Live from Worktown Festivals in Bolton, Lancashire.

Title: *Chuang Tse's Caterpillar.*

Roll up, roll up, get yours while stocks last
A genuine, never-to-be repeated offer
It's not bankrupt stock, they're not counterfeit
Your final chance, tomorrow they'll be gone.

It wasn't meant to end like this.
He was supposed to make a couple of charges
Singe my beard
And I was supposed to smack him on his shoulder
Where the scales are thickest.
He'd roar, she'd scream
I'd sweep past and with one hand
Lift her onto the nag.

There was a big crowd that day.
I knew it was going to go wrong
I had this feeling all day
Under-rehearsed.

It was the knave's fault
I told him not to tie the rope too tight.
She ends up still tied to the post, half-naked
I'm on the ground clutching a handful of white chiffon
And there he lies impaled
On a ten-foot red and white barber's pole.

He left me with a haunting look
As if to say "Georgio, you bastard, I thought we were mates"
Then it was over. Me thinking "What now?"
The last bloody dragon in Christendom.

Ah well, every cloud and all that.
Today's Market Day, the tourist charas are arriving.

Roll-up, roll up, buy three, get one for free
Genuine designer dragon-skin bags
A never to be repeated offer
Tomorrow they'll be just a memory.

Tomorrow and Tomorrow and Tomorrow

Do not presume to tell me how to age
I'll do what I can do to stay his hand
Put porridge in the hour glass to replace the sand
Do not attempt to put me in a cage

Do not pretend that life is more than *just a bowl of ferrets* *
I'll do what I can do to duck death's icy gaze
Wear shades and scuttle in the undergrowth
Do not presume to tell me how to age

Do not insist the master jester of this absurd universe
Has any purpose other than mere malice
That he thinks more of the stable than the palace
Do not insult me with your fairy tales or worse

Do not attempt to lock me in your shed
From here on in the dice man's calling all the shots
Bring out the booze, the fat cigar, the pot
Let me sparkle, let me burn; tomorrow is light years ahead.

* A phrase from *Poetic Off Licence* by Hovis Presley [Flapjack Press, 2015].

Voices Off

Dry today with a powder blue sky
A low sun paints rubber plant shadows on the back wall
I ignore the 'to do' list and read to John Coltrane
You should be outside on day like this voices my mother
Got his nose stuck in a book again mutters my father
I could be sweeping up fallen leaves
Brushing the muddy path
Raking the moss
A fire perhaps to glorify a windless winter day
But no, I stick with my book
The 'to do' list hovering on my shoulder
There are times here when even the sun can try
To make you feel guilty.

LAURA TAYLOR

"One of the country's finest poets, both on the page and on the stage."
Attila the Stockbroker, poet

Laura has challenged arbitrary forms of authority all her life and understands fully the potency of kindness in a world intent on creating division.

Obsessed with words and language since her early childhood, she believes in the power of poetry as a means by which silent voices speak and hidden ears listen, and that books really can be your best friends.

Titles: *Kaleidoscope*
& *Fault Lines.*

Liberty Chant

Read this book.
Read this book.
Read this book again.
Read this book today.
Read this book tomorrow.
Read this book at playtime.
Read this book at bedtime.
Read until the spine is broken.
Read until the school term's over;
in the summer holidays,
in the winter holidays,
in the Easter holidays,
every weekend.
This book is your best friend.
Read until you feel okay,
until the tremble fades away.
Read because your name's inscribed.
Read and fill the space inside.
Read until your knots untangle;
thumbing pages, blanking anxious.
Read so you don't have to speak.
This book's a stopper for your ears.
Hold it when you walk to school.
Read until your embers cool.
Read this book to ruin shame
just like you read it yesterday.
Wrap yourself in blanket words,
wallowing in other worlds,
drench your mind in chapter, verse,
with saturated syntax.

Read until you reach sixteen.
Keep on reading when you leave.
Read this book for liberty.

And when you've finished this,
read another and another
and another and another,
for your knowledge
equals power.

Just Relax

Down at Tit-Squash Central,
we're waiting for our scans.
Our tops are off and on and off
and on and off again.
Our boobs are lubed and drawn on,
we're told to *just relax*,
then tits are clamped securely
within the X-ray's grasp.

My boobs are horizontal now
and flatter than before.
It feels as though they might explode,
I think they've gone too far.
They shouldn't be this shape at all,
a sort of compact disc.
Never mind the atom,
I think me tits are gonna split!

Good god, release the teatery!
Unlock this vile machinery!
Surely this cannot be right?!
I want to scream, I want to fight.
Release the left! Release the right!
Unleash my tender breasticles!

Eventually the beast unclamps.
My bosom is disgruntled.
I comfort them and weigh them up,
just to check they haven't shrunk,
imploded, done a bunk on me,

then shuffle to the waiting room,
sit down with poorly battered baps
and do my best to *just relax*
but next time

I might just punch some fucker's lights out.

Evolutions

A girl born back to front
faces forward now, ahead.
Two times independence
flavours freedom bittersweet.
Each dawn a tender flame
of days to come.

Feel the strings of pinnies past
loosen in the freeze-frame
of our liminality.
The clock's thick tock
shrinks the minutes,
quickens hours,
grows the greying of a winter,
springs the blossom from a seed.

She leaves behind
a blanker space,
bigger house,
empty page;
sunlight cupped in time.
I sidle past the new spare room,
dare to ride the threshold;
write a new space
in the silence.
Each dawn a tender flame
of days to come.

BEN MELLOR

"A pure undiluted talent. Concentrated."
Lemn Sissay MBE, poet

Ben is writer, performer and facilitator who has worked in theatres, festivals, schools, colleges and prisons nationally and internationally.

He has created seven touring theatre shows incorporating spoken word, storytelling, theatre, music, beatbox and vocal looping.

As a facilitator and director, Ben has worked with hundreds of people of all ages and backgrounds in schools, colleges, universities, theatres, community centres and prisons. He has worked in partnership with venues and organisations such as Apples & Snakes, Contact, The Lowry, The Royal Exchange, Manchester Literature Festival and Shakespeare Schools Festival.

Ben has featured on BBC Radio 4, 4 Extra, the World Service and a variety of poetry podcasts, and is a former BBC Radio 4 Slam Champion and winner of the Dike Omeje Slam Poetry Award.

He is currently Youth Theatre Director with Collective Encounters.

Titles: *Light Made Solid*
& *Anthropoetry.*

How to Smash a Piano

First, play it for the last time;
A basic jazz progression
Taught to you by the son
Of your dad's ex-lover,
Played inexpertly
But with heart.

Next, take a sledgehammer
And a deep breath,
Raise both above your head
And bring them down with
What force you can muster,
Smashing the echoes
Of childhood fingers
Playfully tickling the keys.

You'll need a few good swings
To make an impact
For, despite your child-like
Relish of the opportunity
To destroy something beautiful
And your adult rationalisations
That this is the cheapest, safest
And most efficient way
To dispose of an instrument
Not fit for use nor restoration,
Your muscles still scream that
This is wrong
As you reluctantly heft
The hammer's weight.

Get a friend to help.
They will strike with more force,
Decisively delivering blows
Exposing its inner skeleton,
Swiping away supports
Until all that's left
Is a pile of splintered wood,
Broken keys
And a still beating metal heart,
Strings attached.

Keep two of the blue notes –
One for you, one for your sister.
Take the rest to the tip,
Abandoning its cotted iron pacemaker
Behind the skip meant only for wood
Like a baby on a doorstep.

Record it all
On a camera, a hard drive,
Your head and heart.

That you made something from this
Will be all that enables you
To bear the destruction.

Theresa's Dream

Go to sleep, please don't weep my sweet nation,
Renewed brooms will sweep away injustice, just be patient
We'll swell your sagging pride taut with reflation,
Bring you a British dream to make you wake with elation –

So dream Britain! Of a lasting job that pays a fair wage,
Dream your kids will go to schools that are the best of their age,
Dream you won't have to sell your house, live in a square cage
When against the dying of the light you can no longer bear rage.

Then dream that as your life recedes forever in the past
Each successive generation will do better than the last,
But not through welfare mind-states where the beggar plies his craft,
From our temple not the lenders but the debtors shall be cast

To make way for the wealth-creators, risk-takers and innovators
Who'll warm up this frozen economy and be the liquidators
Trickling down golden showers of jobs, homes, cars – key indicators!
This nation's heart's arrested, we will be its defibrillators!

Now is not the time to dream small, be all timorous.
Let's raise towers of ambition erected by fiscal stimulus!
For when it seems the very greatest barriers prohibit us
We'll discover our capacity to rise to challenges is limitless –

This is what we're in this for, this is our reason for being,
The thing that drives us on, our entire cohesion of seeing;
To open hearts, if not doors, to the poor, the beaten and fleeing,
Let them come to their own rescue as we enjoy a season of skiing!

But we admit there are those for whom the dream seems out of reach,
There are even those whose leaders they would like now to impeach,
Hand a big P45 to those they deem to flout and breach
The social contract, but we won't, don't doubt my speech,

We're [*cough*] excuse me [*cough*] I've got some words stuck in my
    throat,
We're throwing out a lifeline to those who [*cough*] choke and struggle
    to float,
Who don't even own their own home let alone a duck house on
    a moat
Or who don't have a home at all, although they don't fucking well
    vote.

No, I'm sorry, this dream is one of equality for all.
I dream when we announce them that our policies enthral
the masses, that it's *Bravo!* not *Hypocrisy!* they call,
I dream our economy won't stall, I dream democracy won't fall

And George may have a gun, but apparently I'm a dead woman
    walking
And you can't kill the living dead so these corridors of power I'll keep
    stalking
And if the ghost of Frida Kahlo tries to strangle me I'll keep talking;
I don't care if no-one's buying this bankrupt dream I'll keep hawking,

But I'm haunted by a Britannia so cool she's chopped up in bags in
    the freezer
And the geezer that did it's coming for us and he's packing a heater
And he's all covered in blood from shooting and stabbing the
    Speaker.
How did it all go wrong for Britannia when we were just gagging to
    please her?!

Britannia's broken, braw bricht, bruised, brained –
like a bream braised in bromide belly-up in brackish brine, *brrr*!
Brisket for breakfast, brunch and brupper,
Brecht's Mack knifes Brel's 'Ne Me Quitte Pas' in the back – et tu,
    Brute?
Brash brigands in braces, brogues and briefcases from Brussels to
    Bruges,
badly bred and broody bros, brokers abrasive as brillos bearing the
    brunt
bringing bribes for old Brock, bugger Basil Brush, *broom broom*!
Brook no brouhaha a braying bitches brew, bras burning,
britches brimming with bragging brats, *brap brap*, eat your bran
    flakes,
brush up on your braille, brasso in your briefs, brilliant bright brittle
    Britannia,
Brand of the brave, breadsticks mean breadsticks,

building a country that works for everyone
building a country that works or everyon
 uilding a count   hat orks for veryon
 uildin a c unt   ha ork or veryo
  ild   unt   at or   o   er

CATHY CRABB

"Nails life every time."
Matt Panesh AKA Monkey Poet, Edinburgh Festival Fringe Society

Cathy is an award-winning playwright and poet who has written extensively for the stage.

Her plays include *Beautiful House, Moving Pictures, Something Right, Beyond the 4th Wall* and *The Bubbler,* and her collaboration with Punam Ramchurn, *Rumba Bar,* premiered in 2018. She has also co-written two musicals with Lindsay Williams and Carol Donaldson, *Dreamers* and *Meat Pie, Sausage Roll.*

Cathy's poetry features on sculptures by Emma Hunter at the former site of Elk Mill in Chadderton, the last mill to be built in Lancashire.

Titles: *Beside the See-Side*
& *MUMB.*

i. Kitchen Sink Haiku

You will never peel
the same potato again.
Alas, more will come.

ii. Car Park Philosophy Haiku

Disabled spaces
are a sign of how we care;
don't' moan about them.

iii. Haiku Deserving of Wine

If I had a pound
for all my wrong decisions
I'd spend it on booze.

Tomorrow

This is the first time I've been sober on a Sunday since '94
I'm exaggerating for imagery effects
It's unusual though; I still deserve a medal

I've decided that the best way to get off fags and booze
is to imagine I have Stockholm syndrome
You do the metaphor

Yes
I've made roll-ups
from ashtray dimps
Yes
I've woken in an unknown bed/town/country
But it hasn't been all good

Clarity has been like a bath of ice
I've been walking in the countryside
I might remember it
No one's annoyed me
My breath is nice

It's happened
not through willpower
I deny myself nothing
People change

Everyone who falls for the trap is an idiot
They're all Jonas inside the whale
with the occasional limpet outside smoking
I'm on an island of sobriety

Tomorrow is someone's birthday though
You can't miss that

Anyway
it's nothing to do with you

The Tomorrow People

In a mottled limb
is life's prized narrative.
Crooked from a thousand gnarls
pruned in circumstance
clinging to the present walls;
all flesh is grass stained.

Like a graze bleed on genes
she is anybody.
Her muscle memory powers a trike,
her fury makes a mark on a scared cheek,
a girl bends her finger back in class
all because a handsome sailor made a pass.

Yet on the ward, folded with the sheet,
paper thin, delicate flower
presses her thumb and index finger,
lightly feels her ridges and creases
knowing nothing really ceases.

JACKIE HAGAN

"With wit and charm, she manages to make us laugh in the face of adversity."
Matt Fenton, Contact Theatre Artistic Director

Jackie is a multi-award-winning poet, playwright and performer who became a Jerwood Compton Poetry Fellow in 2018 and was nominated for a Women of the World award for effecting social change using spoken word.

She has worked extensively for the British Council, represented the UK in slam poetry in Rio de Janeiro, and was the subject of a Channel 4 documentary short.

Jackie has won Saboteur Awards' Best Spoken Word Show twice, is a Creative Future Literary Award winner, and regularly crops up on BBC Ouch! and BBC Radio 4.

Titles: *The Wisdom of the Jumble Sale*
& *Some People Have Too Many Legs.*

Ward 39

A needle
lies
odd angled
in my vein;
this is my new normal,
nine to five,
the nurses know my name.

We sit on ten big red chairs.

The girl next to me eats a jacket potato
with tuna she has brought from home.
Her mum moans in a salmon coat.

In the chair by the window
an old fella drinks Costa coffee discreetly
(we are not allowed coffee here),
smiles mischievously.

I've always hated sound
and light.
I learnt to
make a disco of myself
until I broke
and broke
until I learnt
to enjoy
being broke.

I figured everyone did that.

This stuff is messing with my taste buds.
Grapes taste like dusty bleach.

The chair by the heater, fit scally lad
with limbs at all angles,
badly bleached balding hair,
knees up to his chest,
furiously texts.

Young girl fidgets politely,
frantic cardigan,
reads but never turns the page.
Water bottle with a cucumber infusion centre.
Seeds.
Different box of seeds.
Small book.
Newly diagnosed.

My gums feel off,
like hitting your funny bone.

Opposite me,
a threadbare Alan Bennett,
staring, very ill. Scaring everyone.
Late stages.
I go to the toilet a lot, unplug my machine
and wheel it next door.
In there people wait,
they watch me like I am not real,
I am a spectre of their future.
On the way back I peep into the room next to mine,
the lights are dimmed,
there are beds.

My body feels
like nails
on a blackboard.
This off-white room
is too colourful for my eyes.
My tummy quivers.

A narky woman
wears her sleep
deprivation as a badge of honour.

My fury-cold nurse
does a comedy impression of me,
all scouse and far too hot.
Like a tiny moment from a fever dream.
Like home.

The boy in the chair right next to me
holds himself like high school is still with him,
the bitter bones of a sparrow,
lightness lost.
I want someone to love him,
be gentle with him.

The chair next to the door.
Empty plot.
Little sign *I am clean*.

I can see my pulse
in my vision
like pebbles dropped into a pond,
I can feel my bones in my fingers.

The girl behind has
satisfaction from life
living down to her expectations.

I am wearing sunglasses,
headphones,
earplugs,
eye mask
masking taped
right on my shocked little eyes.
I teach other patients
how to press the buttons
to stop their machines from beeping.
Every day my senses are becoming more heightened,
like a wolf
on acid
with PMS.
I can smell
things that haven't happened yet,
fish before it's caught,
raspberries before they're opened,
I can smell the past;
the person who sat in this chair before me
had an unhappy vagina.

I have started craving clay.
I am willing to pay a lot
to feel the air
in a cave.

I want new things.
They are not impressive.
They are subtle, murky smells in dark places.

I am taking a year off
of not many years
to feel the quality of air in old mills,
sit near a really old tree
and smell myself.
My vision jitters and can't be trusted like an old TV,
there's a specific tone of sound I hear
that feels like I am breathing it.

This chair.
Weird orange haired girl
keeps threatening to throw up
and asking for wet towels,
creeping people out by watching them.
The light continues to scrape.

A Nice Butty

"There are only two ways to live your life: as though nothing is a miracle, or as though everything is a miracle." – Albert Einstein

"Valentine's Day was invented to sell things,
it's a construct to feed capital—"
Shut up!
A billion things are!
Everything is something
that makes you buy shit.
From our standards of beauty
to our notions of 'fun',
the rest of our values
are social control
rooted in injustice
and hungover
from a past
that no longer serves us
and the rest of it is endearingly
unstoppable
tribal
thinking.
So stop,
find a way
through that
allows others to enjoy things.
Imbue meaning in
the way the sunlight catches
on mirrored buildings,
the onset of spring,
the wonky bravado of teenagers,
the buttery taste of shortbread.

Celebrate others
and the small victories,
the simple intimacy of strangers at bus stops,
your increasing ability to be yourself,
the emotional strength of the physically weak,
a nice butty
with just the right ratio of cheese to bread,
the soft secret way
sarcastic gits speak
to their loved ones
when they think you aren't looking,
the simple miracle of existence,
the feel of your breath,
the complex heap of everything you have survived
and all the tiny moments of joy you've created.
Know in your heart
that most of everything is bullshit
and enjoy the absurdity
and the 'tryingness' of humans
and let the silly bastards buy their cards
and struggle to express
the beautiful and heartbreaking
notion of attachment to people
we know will one day die,
let the bastards buy their bleedin' roses.
Let people be.
Life is hard
and we're all going to die
and the sun is shining
and we all ache
to belong and be loved
and you're breathing.

THICK RICHARD

"Stu-fucking-pendous!"
Dr John Cooper Clarke, poet

Thick Richard has been peddling his potty-mouthed punk poetry since the turn of the century.

He has supported John Hegley, Kate Tempest, Jerry Sadowitz, Arthur Smith, The Fall and (sort of) Dr John Cooper Clarke, performed on BBC Radio 4 and presented Radio 6 Music's *Beat of the Day.*

He was co-host of Bang Said the Gun: Manchester and premiered his one-man show, *Swear School*, in 2016 before touring nationally.

Title: *Vaudavillain.*

January January

Vaguely to the tune of 'Heroes and Villains' by the Beach Boys.

I don't remember much of Christmas
Now it only exists in the pixelated pictures
Captured on mobile phones
And thrown around the globe
Through communities of people that I'm never going to know
This year came and passed in a flash
Each one faster than the last
I guess I'll never grasp the speed at which times passes

January January
31 days too long
I can't take another one of those months
Because it smells like last year's laundry
Appalling
Picked up off the floor
Febrezed and worn again
We're all still the same
We wear the same stains
We share the same shame
And then just pass the blame on like a fat one

Because I've spent every year so far
Dancing like a pissed chimp into the future
Naïve and blind to what it might hold
And totally sick and fucking tired of the old one
So the new year begins
With a gurning grin
Turning from hero to villain
At the flick of a cig

These half-remembered January waking dreams
Chased through the cemetery naked and screaming
Time unravels like a bandage revealing
Something you really did not want to see

I remember singing a song
At the top of my lungs
And swinging a punch
At someone I thought had done me wrong
I thought I gave him what for
I'm looking in a broken mirror
With blood on my paw
And now
Sitting in the back of a cab I found out
I'd lost all of my cash down the back of your couch
And he kicked me out

I thought it may be time to reflect and take stock
So I got up
Got my get up on
And got drunk
With the idiots itching
For it all to begin again
Who've waited twelve months
To count down backwards from 10

January January
Here it comes
5
4
3
2
Happy New Year every
1

Noir Was the Night

The neon lights outside
Flashed the bedroom black and white
And the venetian blinds
Cast her sleeping body with zebra stripes

He waited till the seagulls started screaming in the morning
Slipped from her sleeping arms
And silently got dressed
Stepping back into his strides
Pulling on his jacket
With two slow heavy punches
And tying on his tired old shoes
He fixed his hat on his head
Swilled his mouth with the last swallows of whisky and left

Opening the door he paused
And turned to watch her pretend to sleep once more

Stood silhouetted in the hallway light
He tapped a cigarette
From the almost empty deck
Tossed it straight into his lips and struck a light

"I'll see you around doll..." he growled

"Maybe not today...
Maybe not tomorrow...

But it'll 'ave to be one or the other coz I'm back in work Thursday."

ANNA PERCY

"Extraordinary, delicious and passionate."
Janet Rogerson, poet

Anna was born and educated in Norfolk,
but has lived in Manchester for the last decade.

In 2010, she co-founded Stirred, Manchester's influential
pro-feminist collective which organises poetry performances
and writing workshops.

Anna is currently studying for a PhD with a Creative-Critical Project
focusing on her experiences of Bipolar Disorder and Eco Poetry at
Manchester Metropolitan University.

Titles: *Livid Among the Ghostings* &
(co-authored with Rebecca Audra Smith) *Lustful Feminist Killjoys.*

I'd lose all my stamps or Royal Mail would lose the cards or a man drunk from the closing down pub on the corner (the King's Head there's always a King's Head) would piss on all my missives and my want of you would all be wasted I could write you postcards from my home city the ironic crap tourism ones from Norwich with puppet man who still lives and dances with his balding hand puppets and marionettes with a tape deck I could send you postcards from Manchester I would make my own show you the beautiful graffiti Bowie with a secret in the Northern Quarter the Remain posters in the windows how the whole area was thronged by Vote Labour signs before the general election and I felt hope today I am worried I will struggle to send you postcards from anywhere but England after tomorrow there will be no more postcards shaped like the Eiffel Tower the Leaning Tower of Pisa and I will not be able to drink champagne Kir Royales eat Reblochon and the borders will all require visas and I could no longer decide to pick up a copy of the Rosetta Stone and live among the light and eat red peaches in the Loire Valley.

Nocturne

Last night I dreamed she broke in.
She'd know how to elbow a window,

dreams erase the need for ladders.
She took the notebooks from my shelves.

Although we haven't spoken in years
I conjured her mocking tones, wholesale

vitriol distorted by distance and sleep.
She tore off strips of my scrawl, vicious,

rolling them up with great ceremony
in my nocturnal subconscious.

She did what she always did on waking.
While laughing she ate my words.

Now

There is no such thing as past or future we are moving through the everlasting now there is a now where my hair shone long to my waist there is a now coming up where I will need to pare my nails the upturned toes hitting the inside of my black leather Converse there is a now when I woke in the arms of someone whose heart was perfectly joined to mine for a given unit of now however impossible that is there is a now where my skin healing capabilities will slow the burst blister on my heel took less than a week that now is not now there is a now when my skin will no longer feel soft after I brush it in the bath and I will not smell the roses there is a now where I will get a geometric shape burned on me having missed a patch with SPF there is a now when I will have finished writing another book of poetry if I close my eyes I can see the outline of it like persistence of vision there is a now when I will see stars in bed again there is a now where I will successfully paint my fingernails there is a now where I will cycle for an hour with ease there is a now where I am drinking camomile tea this now occurs often there is a now when I will sing on stage again.

MELANIE REES

"Captures the idiocy / wonder / terror of life."
Copland Smith, poet

Melanie is a poet, author and playwright whose play *Drowning Aristotle* won the *City Life* Best of Manchester play award. She co-founded the Pavilion Theatre Company and was Drama Co-ordinator for the Salford Young Person's University.

Born and bred in Salford, her work has recently been anthologised in *Salford Stories* [Bridge House], a collection honouring Shelagh Delaney.

An Associate Lecturer at the University of Salford, trained counsellor and award-winning SEN teacher, she has taught and lived in Australia, India, Israel, Poland and the USA.

Title: (co-authored with Sarah Miller) *Selkie Singing at the Passing Place.*
[Best Collaborative Work runner-up at the Saboteur Awards.]

He didn't consider it an act of terrorism
                              She did
He didn't consider it at all
                              She had
the moment she heard the stage-whisper of his B-29

How long does it take to flip a switch and smile?

    Thirty seconds?
    Twenty seconds?
    Ten?

No, it's the time it takes a man to inhale

    She clambers naked out of Bikini Lagoon
where she has been swimming on that hot
so very hot July afternoon
fumbles for her white shift dress on the sand
looks straight into the prophet's fear
thinks she hears him say *Amen*

    but the prophet is not praying
he's playing rock-paper-scissors inside the cockpit of his plane
    thinking of Gilda
the sketch he stencilled onto the bomb
and the words that read
    For you, Gilda, with love

    She's not yet dead but he's going to make her a corpse
    she holds her breasts to hold in breath

It's against protocol to look down
to the ground
    so he grips at his zipper
        yanks at the fabric to release the strain
            then brain-free
                flips the red switch with his left hand

        drops the Abel bomb

Bikini beach beneath her toes ignites
Mother Earth seems to stutter, shudder
    mutter incomprehensible words
    like money and military operations
        The lagoon hiccups in temper
    spits up fish-heads and rage
        A shade of shrapnel hits her wrist
    melts her bones to synthetic cage
        She screams and the pilot hears show tunes

    Put the blame on Mame, boys
    put the blame ...

    He looks down from his super fortress in LSD trance
sees a naked woman appear to dance on the sand
    and with her brunette curls covered in red contaminated dirt
she reminds him of someone else

He inhales
wishes he had never looked back
    He will never ever tell his grandson Jackson the Third
it was an act of terrorism

        She would have

Had she lived to be a grandmother
Had she lived to see tomorrow
Had she lived just three minutes more

    Nobody listens
to unbearable tales of glistening
so she blows a kiss to the mushroom-shaped mist
    swan-dives into death

She's Rita Hayworth
She's a goddamn bombshell

John McCarthy at the Monastery

He speaks of civil war and riot
beneath a white blue-eyed bearded prophet.
For fifty minutes he speaks
on a lectern but never mentions a god,
only humanity.

Standing below a bronze cross
he remembers shapes,
a spiral staircase, the accusing finger
of a rifle edge, his last horizon
before the blindfold stole the sun.

The hard gold chairs of the monastery
make my spine throb
as he remember textures,
a sack, a foam mattress,
concrete walls and the smart of unknown
knuckles rapped across his skull.

The blue-eyed prophet's head leans to the right,
John McCarthy's to the left
as he remembers taste,
bread and cheese, a jug of water,
the parched mouth from the gruesome
routine of watching shadows dance under the door.

He takes a sip of water from a plastic bottle.
I cross, uncross, then cross my legs
as he remembers smells,
masking tape, diesel fuel,
the scent of second guessing.

An altar candle blows out
as he speaks not of his captors' guilt
but of his own
and he remembers conversations,
how they painted the walls of the cell
with their future,
a trip to Argentina, a family meal,
his first pint.

In Gorton monastery on a windy Thursday,
beneath a blue-eyed bearded prophet,
for fifty minutes he speaks
on a lectern but never mentions a god,
only humanity.
For himself.
For those that kept him in chains.

And I do not offer up a prayer
to the beauty of the monastery,
but take out my notebook and I write.

Prophet

I watch as the prophet's eyes change colour
Blue to green to brown to blue
ever-changing like the kaleidoscope
I got for Christmas when I was four

This prophet has no gender
oscillates between man and woman
appearing first as my red-haired mother
in '80s tie-dye t-shirt tearing open Tetley teabags
and though I never really believed
her tealeaves readings
I'll always cherish those Sunday mornings
sat in our kitchen wearing dressing-gowns
searching for butterflies in cups

The prophet is then the guru in India
who taught me yoga, anointed my head with oil
said tomorrow was always *just the other side of the door*

Then the prophet becomes the gypsy
who read my tarot cards
in a tatty caravan on Brighton pier

Finally the prophet becomes *him*
standing on my doorstep
September sunshine in his hair
with a bouquet of sunflowers, a smile
a tattoo of a compass on his chest
pointing True North

But sometimes the prophet
is not human but a bird
Six magpies on my garden lawn
promising gold
a lost bat in my attic flat
wafting her wings on wood
a mantra in Morse code
a ladybird on my kitchen counter
a spider in my shoe

Sometimes the prophet is simply a horoscope
read from a crumpled paper on the bus
a fortune cookie
a single white feather found
a tension headache on a full moon

Tired of false prophets, charlatans and lies
I close my eyes
to open my sixth chakra
and in the abyss I see
the sky, the stars, a pale blue dot
the Earth from four billion miles away

I inhale through rounded mouth
hold – exhale slowly
Know it is I who is the prophet

STEVE O'CONNOR

"Sensitive but secure … mature yet subtle."
Robert Cochrane, The Bad Press

Steve is a Mancunian living in West Yorkshire, where he teaches creative writing at colleges and libraries and runs bespoke distance learning courses.

He devised and co-hosted Freed Up, which revolutionised the Manchester poetry scene, worked with Write Out Loud and transformed their Trafford-based poetry open mic night, and co-edited all three volumes of the *Best of Manchester Poets* anthologies.

Steve wants more people to write; it's his mission in life.

Title: *extraño.*

Zukunft

Ornaments feel nothing
Photos don't gaze back
Unread diaries catch fast
Memory unwraps

All mirrors embarrass
Doors are best left shut
Visitors intrude
Kind words are not enough

Cups of coffee go cold
Skin remains unwashed
Phone continues ringing
It all comes to a cost

You ask for tomorrow
It isn't mine to give
Both of us are crying
But neither forgives.

Birdsong

Traffic hums like an approving parent
Captivated by other pursuits
Oblivious to the sport of birds
Flitting between branches and singing
The history of the trees
Each high whistle a story of blossom falling
Sweet scented spring rain
Or a season's stray eyelash brushed away
By warmer days

Beneath a hot swell of scrutiny
The bark creaks and a feast gushes
From the gash – a Dionysian pantry
Of bugs, beasts and other treats
To fill the beaks and stomachs
Of hungry hatchlings
Vomit soup nurtures those who cling
To the nest – a famished chorus
A greedy, needy nursery

And the low notes tell a tale of darker days
Invaders fought until blood fell from the sky
Gives warning of territory
And of a time a grimalkin climbed the tree
Spitefully slashing and dashing the youngest
To the unforgiving concrete
White spatters around the roots
Amassed like years of paint
Spilled carelessly

In each bird's song there is a legend
That transforms to symphony. It dips and rises
Like a descent of hollow-boned bodies
Hearts fluttering in air pockets
This chaotic genealogy –
Recurrent origins that dare to grow from shoots
Exposed to nature's cruelty
Holds fast to the footpath
And will one day silence the motorway.

Communication

In an airport lounge
language flits between a mother
and a son.

"When will it come?" the son asks.
The bud of his mother's mouth folds.

HENRY NORMAL

"Dovetails bittersweet poetry with a sublimely observant wit."
The Guardian

Henry is a writer, poet, TV and film producer, founder of the Manchester Poetry Festival (now the Manchester Literature Festival) and co-founder of the Nottingham Poetry Festival.

In 1999, he set up Baby Cow Productions, executive producing all and script editing many of the shows of its seventeen-and-a-half-year output during his tenure as MD. He was honoured with a special BAFTA for services to television in 2017.

Since retiring in 2016, Henry has written and performed five BBC Radio 4 shows, *A Normal Family*, *A Normal Life*, *A Normal Love*, *A Normal Imagination* and *A Normal Nature*, combining comedy, poetry and stories about bringing up his autistic son.

Henry was recently given an Honorary Doctorate of Letters by Nottingham Trent University and has also had a beer named after him.

Titles: *Staring Directly at the Eclipse*, *Travelling Second Class Through Hope*, *Raining Upwards*, *This Phantom Breath*, *The Department of Lost Wishes* & *Swallowing the Entire Ocean*.

Infinity Minus One

Sunbathing in winter
only the moon is getting tanned

Just shy of eternal love
One step towards home

I look back on the unimaginable
decorated with ribbons

Consciousness dapples

I am absurd
in debt

I have no dance to amuse strangers
I am a wishbone unpulled

a tombstone pending
a rogue planet at best

To my right in the dark
a lucky number lies on its side

My son counts down time with
a stopwatch on the sand

Oblivion Sounds a Bit Heavy Metal for D.H. Lawrence

Oblivion is truly democratic
Admirably consistent in logic

Promises nothing it can't deliver
Can't be bought or blackmailed or bargained with
Can't be conned, bullied or even betrayed

Oblivion cures all pain in its embrace
Unburdens all responsibility
It clears space for new possibilities
It redistributes all intrinsic wealth

Oblivion's inevitable, and no
more unwelcome in any universe
than either the consistent speed of light
the creation of hydrogen or the
implausible wonder of life itself

For Those of Us Who Were Once Useful

On even the greyest of days
you can light a candle

and there seems something healthy
every once in a while about not washing

I'm uneasy sharing the step with ants

There are more of them than
I can keep an eye on

There appears to be two sizes
neither of which I'd like inside my clothes

Both scales share a sense of urgency
though each individual insect rushes in a different direction

I'm unsure whether they are scouting new ground
or revisiting terrain already explored

If I follow any single traveller
there is no straight line but
like a shopping trolley
with a faulty wheel
it veers and corrects

For the most part these creatures
avoid contact with each other

I would like to pretend I have
somehow earned the opportunity for love

or that my inherent virtue
deserves a conspiracy of fate

but I guess chance and good fortune
are just names we give
the chain of events we enjoy

Self-flattery
musing
on morality and just desserts

Do I believe in destiny?
I was born to answer that question

and the answer is
no

REBECCA AUDRA SMITH

"An absolute joy ... raucous, provocative, tender, funny and sexy."
Judy Gordon, Write Out Loud

Rebecca comes from Gloucestershire, but enjoys being an honorary Mancunian.

She competed in the Anti Slam Final Heat 2015 representing Manchester, and the Superheroes of Slam final 2015.

Rebecca co-founded Stirred with Anna Percy, Manchester's influential pro-feminist collective which organises poetry performances and writing workshops.

Title: (co-authored with Anna Percy) *Lustful Feminist Killjoys.*

Morning

In the morning we can start over.
We'll pick our clothes off the floor and fit arms into sleeves,
we will gather up the memorabilia and junk it,
wash away the scent of the bed in the shower.

We'll pick our clothes off the floor and fit arms into sleeves.
The way last night we fit into each other,
wash away the scent of the bed in the shower.
The morning has arrived and put us asunder.

The way last night we fit into each other
like a body under sand, the contours shift.
The morning has arrived and put us asunder,
like a bed in an ocean, we are set adrift.

Like a body under sand, the contours shift,
it makes no sense to remember how we kissed.
Like a bed in an ocean, we've been set adrift,
we've not understood love, how difficult it is.

It makes no sense to remember how we kissed.
In the morning we can start over,
we've not understood love, how difficult it is.
We will gather up and burn our memorabilia.

My Body Could Be an Ocean if You Would Let Me Swim

You could be mermaid they said,
grow your hair to reach your tits,
seaweed-fine, straightened shine,
wet sea-spray gloss.

If anything it is an anchor, dragging me
to bow my head to the ground, groom it,
weigh me down, the tide tug at my toss,
sit on a rock-ritual, brush brush brush.

Look in the mirror and practise your song,
salt in your mouth, the taste of compliments
bitter as oysters, the suck of them on your teeth
as you chuck it back, *thanks.*

Launch me into the ocean of my body,
rock me within the meeting of our two skins,
we can wear our faces like disguises,
we can make pet names for each other –

just don't separate my breasts and individually
name them like a species of bird you have found
that you cup, at once gentle and possessive.
This body of mine is not treasure hunting.

I will preserve myself in brine,
like sailors at sea would eat salt biscuits.
They say they would go crazy for women,
alone for months at the ocean's sway;

they say they would go mad.

PAUL NEADS

"Publishes the most cutting-edge poetic performers."
Writing Manchester

Paul is the founder and commissioning editor of Flapjack Press.

Aside from Flapjack's regular output, he also oversees the production of publications for schools, workshop groups, charities and other publishers, and helps to set up independent publishing houses in a vague consultancy role.

An exhibiting artist and illustrator, he has provided the art for several in-house publications, including Tony Walsh's *I Can Draw My Alphabet* and Dommy B's children's books and theatre shows.

His own poetry and short stories have appeared in numerous magazines and anthologies, under numerous pseudonyms, the truth only coming out when he's had to admit his identity to get any of the somewhat rarer-than-numerous payments.

Subsistence for Existence

The rain has gone now
leaving damp earth to bleed into the horizon,
a turquoise sky, Payne's grey cloud
and everything becomes a cut-out.

Colour in between the outlines
with charcoal thoughts, stand back
to watch the night.

Focus blurs in this expanse,
a throw-over to hide infinity
and inability to comprehend
is met with silence.
Perspective
bound by constraint.

Overhead clears.
A dusting of early stars,
lower a planet or two.

Venus and Mars.
Love and War.
Sex and Death.
Onwards and upwards.

Or maybe down.

Reversal of Fortunes

I, Edward Mordake, being of unsound body
and unsound of mind, do hereby give notice
of my intention to die.

Born God-blighted heir to the noblest peerage,
defiled by a demon face, the parasitic twin
'pon the back of my head,

whilst forward Antinous, sight set beyond
horizons of each and every day yet to come
bears the liminal torture of carnival Janus.

This slayer of intellect, reason and worth,
designer of the curse that has set my path
to retrograde, devouring my tomorrows

in knowledge of my immoral inbreeding,
arcane to the pure, sinister and curious to all,
grants me no peace.

The balm of sleep does not prevail, for its lips
gibber without ceasing with a sneer and a smile
whilst I weep, whispering throughout the night
such things they only speak of in hell.

No sotto sweet-nothings, no guiding voice
in the dark to calm and lead across a feather-crack
too broad to span; my paradox,

my nature of being, my presence a disjunction,
the two-faced man and bait of glass-housed voyeurs
who recoil at first fright

then a relief and release I will never know, glad
they are not so, and laugh that it is I, not them,
who has paid the price.

And although they may leave by dusk each day
I am never alone, for throughout the night,
the whispering, forever the whispering,
the taunt of my greatest fear:

I, Edward Mordake, being of unsound body
and unsound of mind, do hereby give notice
of my intention to live.

JOHN DARWIN

"Visceral, delicate, vulnerable and utterly engrossing."
Matt Abbott, poet

John thought he was a poet from birth but was kicked into action by his Dad's terminal illness and a desire to do something more than shifting papers and supping pints.

He was the host of Write Out Loud's poetry night in Sale for two years, a member of the critically acclaimed touring troupe A Firm of Poets for a couple more, and is co-host at Spoken Weird in Halifax.

He lives, drinks, loves and laughs in Prestwich, North Manchester.

Title: *I Meet Myself Returning.*

The Way That She Left

Tomorrow we'll eat only vitamin pills,
sculpt our faces on virtual screens,
enter friendships on scores out of ten,
leave them emotionless
but still won't know when;

know when we're dying
to the nearest half day,
appreciate living
in a Stepford Wives way,
cry only when ordered,
laugh not at all,
pay full disregard to the homeless,

make plans for living
without colour or joy;
hear soft shuffle footsteps
with no longing or regret
for her signature sound,
the way that she left.

Statue of You

Yesterday I burned your clothes on a pyre.
Today I pretend that nobody knows.
Tomorrow, commission a statue of you,
on a plinth in the bedroom, to help me get through.

Crafted of copper
by hands made of steel
in sub-zero temperature,
so we cannot see

the lips that are sealed,
the arms that are crossed.
The feet I was wooed with
on the statue are lost.

We stole time from working
in a bed in the Lakes.
In a dull Midlands town
we turned love to heartbreak.

You asked me to whistle
some Troubadour's song
to keep you amused
while you strung me along.

We all know that real men
are fearless and strong.
The time was half right.
The place was half wrong.

Carp Fishing in Shropshire

I could go carp fishing in Shropshire.
Pitch a tent with a quart of spirits,
fish through the night
taking occasional sips
and a gulp with each bite.

I could walk five miles to town,
stroll from book shop to library,
taking in architecture,
supping water to stop night cramps
with a late small tincture for sleep.

I could remedy lost education,
learn Welsh as a family nod,
wander far and wide
chatting aimlessly to shopkeepers
and passers-by.

I will go to the pub too often,
repeat myself to irritated bar staff.
Fart prolifically without knowing,
forget who I am
and die.

SARAH MILLER

"Better than chocolates."
Cathy Thomas-Bryant, Puppywolf

Sarah is a poet, playwright and theatre deviser with over 30 plays produced and whose poetry can be found carved on stone at Channelside Haven, Barrow-in-Furness.

She has facilitated workshops from South Cumbria to West Africa and worked as a theatre director, writer-in-residence and dramaturg, collaborating with communities, visual artists, dance companies and sonic improvisers.

Sarah is featured in digital composers Hugs Bison's film *Besides* and, with pre-recorded poems, 'virtually' appeared on their *B-Side the Seaside* tour.

Title: (co-authored with Melanie Rees) *Selkie Singing at the Passing Place.*
[Best Collaborative Work runner-up at the Saboteur Awards.]

The Premonitions Bureau

Alarm bells shudder her awake
She picks apart her dreams
Sifting through the ordinary
All isn't as it seems
Strange portents, symbols, signs
Swim in definites, maybes, mights
She takes the moleskin book
And meticulously writes

She scries her swirling tea
Turns the cup to read the leaves
She was a sceptic once
Now, she just believes
Although only employed
To answer the Bureau phone
After months of logging premonitions
She's bringing her work home

She now avoids all ladders
Sidesteps black cats and their paths
Used to think it was all rubbish
Till the Bureau did its maths
Seventy-six replies
About the tragedy of Aberfan
Those who said they'd visions
And could have saved their fellow man

So now the public ring
Tell of tragedies they see
She records, date stamps and files them
Where they're supposed to be

Plane Crash, Natural Disaster,
Assassination, Celebrity Death
She listens to them all
Sobs under her breath

Tomorrow's become her enemy
It's now beyond bad luck
She's no longer making any plans
In case tomorrow stands her up
It may be pseudo-science
But it's got into her head
And she'd logged down the prediction
Seeing Dr Barker dead

Some say it was nocebo effect
Brought on by two of his best
Whose accurate descriptions
Consistently passed all tests
She's scouring the Wanted ads
Knows what she must do
Got to find another job
Before the future kills her too.

In Response to 'Britannia' by Joana Vasconcelos

'Britannia' was part of the artist's exhibition Time Machine *at Manchester Art Gallery.*

Monsters and fantasies,
wild beasts and carnivals,
all breasts and ovaries
teeming to life.

Fur and feathers,
flowers and pom-poms
trim polite drawing rooms
with their enlarged vulvas out.

Tasselled and stretched
into saggy-boobed strippers,
twisting and cha-cha-ing
roots writhing about.

Evolution run riot
in the Petri dish of art.
Makes a northern rainforest
or a Manchester tart.

Escaping old cotton,
layers cutting deep
to embrace hedonism,
in search of its own
glittery bass beat.

GERRY POTTER

"Poems that will amuse, move, inspire and provoke."
Paul Burston, Polari Literary Salon

Gerry is a poet, playwright, director, actor, and both creator and destroyer of the infamous gingham diva, Chloe Poems.

A favourite son of Manchester and his home town Liverpool, he is an Everyman Youth Theatre alumnus and National Museums Liverpool lists him amongst the city's leading LGBTQ+ icons.

His published works are included in both the poetry and philosophy collections at Harvard University, and the portrait documentary *My Name is Gerry Potter* premiered at Homotopia in 2015.

Titles: *Chloe Poems's Li'l Book o' Manchester, Planet Young, Planet Middle Age, The Men Pomes (Because Men Don't Say Poems), Fifty, The Chronicles of Folly Butler, The Story Chair, Accidental Splendour of the Splash & Manchester Isn't the Greatest City in the World: The Rise and Rise of The Bourgeois Zeitgeist.*

The Erosion

Sea in/out,
cycles 'n' roundabouts,
revolutions peaceful pass.
Nature got it right,
anarchy and calm are where it's at,
what it's always been,
filling fish with plastic's a greedy bitch.
The Erosion's us,
we wither 'n' whittle,
architects of splintered goods.
We've wintered every summer with pollution;
fortunate breathe,
unlucky choke.

There's this bloke thinks climate change
is hot money,
struck gold on a car-crashed Barrier Reef.
He's The Erosion,
the end, insane, eye on the dollar
and promotion.
When the commotion's a storm,
there's beauty.
Yeah, a roof blows off, but the sky lights up,
ring-pulls are murdering whales.
Black Friday January sales into the apocalypse,
Disneyland sunsets,
one wing'd or not,
bets are on when the bees are gone.

Nature may occasionally rip up trees,
but we burn them to make plastic packaging for fruit.

Tomorrow Cometh

There's a comfy sofa,
monochrome shaped in yesterday.
Before the seventies,
before glam,
before tripping became compulsory.
I'm on it watching
telly,
shift workers.
Waiting baited breath and spine tight
for pocket money.

I can hear it outside,
the hum,
throb,
rattling clatters of industry.
Rumbling thunders
without dark clouds,
rain.
It feels inside,
sat with me,
sofa'd,
comfy.

Later I'll stand by its braziers,
spark spit fire-cracking,
escaping,
listening to jokes I've heard before.

Tomorrow Came

Apparently the sofas are comfier now,
telly's 3D.
Back of the couch, needles,
under the cushions,
opportunity,
food banks,
AIDS.

ROD TAME

"A tour de force of a poet ... an eloquence on the page,
complimenting his elegant stage presence."
Regie Cabico, Nuyorican Poet Café Grand Slam Champion

Originally from the Garden of England that is Kent,
performance poet, actor and compère Rod Tame
now lives in the urban jungle that is Manchester.

He has hosted and performed regularly at the rich variety
of poetry nights in the area, with the occasional foray
into alien lands, including at the historic Stonewall Inn
during New York Pride.

Title: *Strange World Odd Person.*

Evolution of the Cybermen

The public might scoff but a boffin states
Cybermen will exist within one hundred years from now.
Technically possible, technically-evolved humans – *wow!*
Is it me? Or might this be unwise?

With medical implants
these next-gen men will have senses enhanced.
But Mr Scientist, please, use your common ones to see
the drawbacks in this plan.

People living lives extended,
like a clapped-out banger
having body parts mended,
does not help solve the over-population conundrum
or the pension fund doldrums.

Not to mention the intention
of these mechanic fanatics to rule the world – FOREVER!
Have you NEVER watched *Doctor Who*?!

If you had, you would agree
the obvious conclusion to your scientific spree.
This upgraded form of life
would declare the likes of you and me
obsolete – like analogue TV.

Mother Nature's organic spawn
would, at best, be sub-species pawns.
At worst, a faded blast from the past.
Extinct in the blink of a cyborg's eye.

Except it probably won't blink.
Professor, stop and think!

When tinkering under the biological hood,
do you ever consider whether you should?

Ghost Story

Some kids' monsters aren't under the bed.
In a box room at the landing's end,
Muppets smile over a five-year-old's head.

"Mum, is that you?"

He heard a creak,
a floorboard squeak at the other end
by the stairs.

He asks again,
"Mum, is that you?"

Silence,
another creak, slightly closer.
A step?

Kid's limbs freeze under duvet,
Paddington pattern,
Please look after this bear.
Doesn't dare move a hair,
but listens harder than anybody has ever listened
...to silence.

Arm moves the merest inch,
prompts a foot-falling creak.
Kid breaks a cold sweat,
frets about a ghostly figure
ill-feeling its way along the banister.

A waking nightmare.
Only escape is sleep
but it doesn't come.

Over breakfast cereal bowl,
rumble-tumming,
kid questions Mum
about the spook.

Pouring milk, she pauses.

Hesitates, cogitates,
explains that it's the neighbours
moving around.
Thin walls, old floorboards gossiping.

Mum pours the milk again,
snap, crackle, pop goes the fear.

Twenty years later,
conversation recalls
these spectral imaginings.

Mum hesitates, cogitates,
and confesses to man,
"Actually, I heard those steps too,
so did your Nan."

The little soldier boy inside reels,
squeals, "You lied to me!"

But what was the alternative?

Tell a five-year-old kid
about a ghost working the night shift
outside his bedroom door?
Maybe a malevolent monk,
wringing blooded hands,
or a wailing bride unwedded
or ruffled nobleman beheaded,
but someone undoubtedly dead-ed!
The rotten swine.

Some kids' monsters aren't just in their head
and, sometimes, Mum really does know best.

GENEVIÈVE L. WALSH

"Unique and passionately inclusive."
Steve Nash, poet

Geneviève is a Yorkshire-based poet and the founder and co-host of Spoken Weird, Halifax's monthly open mic, and its LGBTQ+ sister night, Spoken Queered.

After co-creating Stirred's Invisible Disabilities Slam in 2017, she became a core member of their Manchester collective. She has also performed as a member of nationally acclaimed touring troupe A Firm of Poets.

Geneviève is currently developing her first one-woman show, *A Place in the Shade.*

Title: *The Dance of a Thousand Losers.*

...But Satisfaction Brought It Back

Heads turn
as a sentient mass
of matted fur
takes callous strides
on the bypass,
stopping now and then to stretch
with an air of awesome smugness.
A lust
for all nine of her lives.
A strut
so compelling and faultless,
it compliments
the tyre marks.
Symmetrical,
harmonious.

In the choking fogs of ugliness,
satisfaction reigns.
It's pulled her back from the jaws of death
when the fists and knives with her name on came.
That four-by-four that smacked her down
was shrugged off like a papercut,
not a mislaid bead of sweat.
No shame,
no distress,
this pile of fluff and bones
remains proud to be curious.
Still howling at the gridlocked city,
still on all four feet.

Passing cars slow down for a peek,
roll down their windows,
spit
and chide,
the classic British pastime of rubbernecking
satisfied.

This Seething Isle
is breathing piss and venom far and wide
but she's oblivious.
Symmetrical,
harmonious.
To everything but the sound of *Satisfaction*,
she's impervious.

Tomorrow, she will recommence
her decade-spanning dalliance
with the Imp of the Perverse,
front-page stuff
that makes all other flings look tedious.

Whispers and Fists

After 'Lament for the Moth' by Tennessee Williams.

A whisper
has stricken the dancefloor.
They've slipped in through the cracks and vents
en masse, a swarm from the underpass,
a kamikaze mission
with a target on his chest.

The mammoth
spits and dry heaves,
a mess of wing and thorax
breaks the straight, harsh lines
of his breastplate,
petrified in amber nectar,
stark, unbridled hate.

Sing a mournful song for the Mottephobe.
This velvet-on-leather sensation
leaves him groaning with revulsion.
Hear him curse creation
with his final, laboured lungfuls,
wait for the snap of the heart strings.
A sea of twitching carcasses
make every move a fruitless hell,
watch him strike a dated pose
in the face of annihilation.

Lament
for the wounded mammoth,
he's blind to his own extinction.

His pilfered moves
preserved for all eternity in ice,
every beat of our wings
a sarcastic kiss.

A single moth can't take a punch,
but a whisper beats a fist.

Colour-by-Numbers

This is your future
    (colour-by-numbers edition:
    brush and white/beige/pastel paints enclosed).
    Optional vibrancy
    sold separately.

For the sake of your dignity,
stray not from the lines.

Pray not for carbs,
nor wines under £8.99.
No outrageous laughs,
no referring to your home as your 'gaff'.
No more sticky-back tactics,
blu-tac memories on the wall,
no more mismatched emergency chairs,
no more thrift-shop
culture-shock
table-top discord.

Message understood.
I will stand in my hellish migraine of a house
and admit defeat.
I'll commence my megastore goose-step,
pound the floor,
zombie-esque,
all the way from the door to the desk.

Get some nice self-assembly furniture
on which I can shelve my records,

notebooks,
sci-fi knick-knacks,
old magazines
and band t-shirts
and my
very
sense
of
self.

Remove the category of 'life' from my living expenses.
Make a faithful hound of my senses,
command her to heel
and sit
and stay
somewhere between *Mrs Beeton* and *50 Shades of Grey*.

I'll whitewash my frontal lobes,
I'll spellcheck the lyrics in my heart,
I'll Feng Shui my rage.
I'll assemble my flat-pack 2.4
and sleep in an apple-white cage.

Ladylike by proxy,
free of my enlightened toxins.

I'll tick all the boxes.

But in the end, you'll just want your money back.
Because life is colour-by-numbers,
and the only colour in my palette is black.

DAVE VINEY

"One of the authentic voices of Manchester."
Dr Jo Bell, poet

Dave grew up in Stretford, Manchester, and started writing poetry and short stories at the age of 14 (largely in secret – due to a shortage of poets in the area and an excess of people who liked to punch poets in the face).

Co-host of Bang Said the Gun: Manchester and a regular guest at poetry nights across the UK, he has written and performed for BBC Manchester Radio and, as part of Working Verse Collective, written and performed two sell out shows at the Lowry Theatre in Salford.

In 2013, Dave was the Poet Laureate of Kendal Calling Festival and the following year debuted his one man spoken word show, *Shapes*, at the Edinburgh Fringe.

Titles: *The Prequel to the Sequel* (Working Verse Collective; with Kieren King & Benny-jo Zahl) & *A Poet Called Dave.*

The One That Waits in Their Tomorrow

She has [insert insufficient superlative here] eyes
that can steal speech from cocksure mouthpieces
and blind off-guard, foolhardy soul searchers.
A heart in hiding.
Maybe when the bruising goes down.
Holds trust like a hand grenade.
Knows that if it explodes only she will feel it.
Knows because it has.
Frisks compliments for concealed weapons,
and her walls…
her walls are reinforced with solid resolve,
topped with shards of broken promises.

He trips over the darkness of darker days.
Overshares, unaware that he's purging.
Remembers just a moment too late
that not all childhoods were made this way,
but refuses not to cherish the blisters:
pantomimes his past,
acts like audience –
ridicules his villains.

She patents infectious angle-finding;
knows the shape of hustle.
Splashes through conversations like puddles.
Laughs with no pretext, subtext or contest.
Tries to face-pull beauty away, but fails
beautifully.

He is an open book
in a locked box.

Hug-pushes affection to a safe distance.
Feels unbalanced, fogged-up –
waits for her to scrawl her name in his condensation.

They love in radar blips;
near misses on the grid.
Laugh in parallel.
Settle into the thought of each other
like freshly washed sheets,
peripherally aware that if they ever aligned
their shared memories would over time
become soft focus,
accompanied by a button-pushing power ballad
that neither would own up to.

Todaydreamer

Tomorrow's To-do List:

- Command your thoughts;
    relax to the drastic.
    Use a sanity you made earlier
    with sticky-back plastic.

- Buy competitively-priced novelty goods;
    bin the boring and the plain;

    see the world

    through rose-tinted cellophane.

- Be a used-hope salesman
    selling second-hand desires.
    Booby-trap all conversations
    then wait for the crossed wires.

- Duck, dive and freestyle through tricky situations.
    Take a super-scooper pick 'n' mix
    of life's sweetest persuasions.
    Work for stress, low pay and a Molotov Migraine.
    (Still be standing room only on the 7.18 Gravy Train.)

- Be food for thought,
    eat humble pie,
    be a couch potato,
    be the apple of your eye.
    Be crackers.

Dry.

- Make hopscotch compulsory
  for overbearing dads.
  Prove him wrong and punch your way
  out of a paper bag.

- Seek out spoilers on your future.
  Get the drop on Fate's intentions.
  Mystic Margaret sees it all
  and needs a new extension.

- Make todaydreams your reality,
  night-terrors good to go.
  There won't always be a crock of shit
  at the end of every rainbow.

Today's To-do List:

- See tomorrow.

TONY CURRY

"This is our poetry, these are our poems."
Tony Walsh AKA *Longfella*, poet

Tony is a performance poet, playwright, workshop facilitator, soundsmith and enabler.

His solo spoken word shows include *Brit Boy*, *Complicit Relations*, *Moving* and *The Odyssey*, which he performed at Manchester's Royal Exchange Theatre.

Tony is the host of Word Central – Flapjack Press's monthly open mic night at Manchester Central Library – and the Mancsgiving cabaret in Whalley Range, South Manchester.

Titles: *The Noble Savage* &
Tall Tales for Tall Men Who Fall Well Short.

This'll Take the Pain Away

Side-mouthed snarls
Sidles up
Takes his time
The beat is up
The heat is on

Side-mouthed snarls
Sidles up
To wide-mouthed Eddie
And breathes with malice intent

Wide-mouthed Eddie
Stares forlornly
He's been in this scene before
Tugs at his beard
And stares

Two-toothed Tony
Appears
A figure tall and black

Wide-mouthed Eddie
Knows now his time is nearly up
The pair share a smoke
And a joke

Wide-mouthed Eddie
Relaxes and reclines
His mind wanders

The frost is up
He can see his breath
On this golden morning
Jess runs ahead
And he says a *good morning*
To a woman
Sprite
Healthy
In what he thinks
Must be her seventieth year

Jess looks back
He nods
She crosses the bridge

His boots
Click-clank
Click-clank
Click-clank
And it reminds him of a rhythm
He caught the night before

All in time
All in time
All in time
It's all in time
And he thinks of the dark singer
Who smiled and teased at his cumbersome advances
Caught once again in her lair
He'd already touched her
Running his bony finger along her arm
Around her neck
Before licking his finger

Tasting her sweat
Which was *sweet* he said
This made her laugh

She wiped his brow
And he felt her breath
She said
"Don't worry, I can take all of your cares away"

She kissed the tear
Before it fell

Side-mouthed snarls
Places the blade
In the palm of his hand
And stares into Eddie's eyes

"This won't hurt"
She says
"And it'll take the pain away"

He smiles
And doesn't feel the incision
"Thanks"
He says
"I owe you my life"

"We know
Sleep now boy
You've earned it"

There Isn't Anything Permanent

We strive in honest toil
And batten down the hatches
And look to a future made permanent

We try to harness the wind
And lay a veneer of plastic over
Dust and weeds

As the eddies rise and the gates buckle
We lay sandbags and pray

But it's the impermanence that gets me
It's always been the same
We harness and stick in our flags
And give great speeches about hope
People
Prosperity

And we hope
That the show home
And the smiling kids
Will aid our comfort
So we buckle in
Build 'em up
Keep 'em out
To keep us safe

But it's the impermanence that gets me
How these weeds and shit will blow up
How this technological super-age
Is the answer to all

While our kids lose the ability
To be human

And all we've got to show for it
Is our ability to buy a new pair of jeans
Or a door knocker
At four in the morning

And we talk endless endless endless garbage

And while we're attached to plastic blocks
Like our whole life depends on it
Like the believer
Who in past-times
Would have held fast to The Bible
For comfort guidance and joy
Now it's another tablet
Where we never know what's going on
And what they'll say
"Oh really?"

And they sit
With their feet up
And their curvy hair
And their stick-out boobs
And chillax
And bemoan the migrants
Who frankly get on their nerves
And say
"Thinking that they can escape their stuff
To then
Somehow
Take our stuff?
I don't think so"

And I think of the endless endless plastic
And the endless endless metals
And the stuff in tablets
And the screens
And I think of the poor poor
Buggers
Who put it there
Whose homes and lands have been pillaged
So *we* can be safe
Permanent

But we can't ever be permanent
Dummy
Cos we're all skin
Bone
Water
And not much else

And the wind will blow
And the dust will get in our eyes
And the weeds will continue to infect our permanent plans
   We are all impermanent
   Our lives are impermanent
   We are all impermanent
   Our lives are impermanent
   We are all impermanent
   Our lives are impermanent

CHRONOLOGY OF FLAPJACK PRESS PUBLICATIONS

Aaaaaaaaaaaaagh! Dinosaurs! [1]	Dommy B	£7.00
MUMB	Cathy Crabb	£8.00
As in Judy	Rosie Garland	£8.00
No Tigers	Dominic Berry	£8.00
The Dance of a Thousand Losers	Geneviève L. Walsh	£8.00
Colourquest [1]	A.K. McAllister	£9.99
Travelling Second Class Through Hope	Henry Normal	£8.99
Accidental Splendour of the Splash	Gerry Potter	£10.99
Vaudavillain	Thick Richard	£9.99
Raining Upwards	Henry Normal	£8.99
Art By Johnny [2]	Johnny Carroll-Pell	£12.00
Selected moments of machine life	Pete Ramskill	£8.99
Fault Lines	Laura Taylor	£8.00
Staring Directly at the Eclipse	Henry Normal	£9.00
This Phantom Breath	Henry Normal	£10.00
The Department of Lost Wishes	Henry Normal	£10.00
Manchester Isn't the Greatest City …	Gerry Potter	£12.00
I Can Draw My Alphabet [1]	Tony Walsh, Paul Neads	£7.50
I Meet Myself Returning	John Darwin	£7.50
extraño	Steve O'Connor	£8.00
Swallowing the Entire Ocean	Henry Normal	£10.00
The Anthology of Tomorrow	Flapjack Press	£10.00

[1] For children [2] Art collection

Prices correct at time of this book going to print. Flapjack Press reserves the
right to show new retail prices on covers which may differ from those above.

Available in paperback and eBook from www.flapjackpress.co.uk.

To receive advance information on forthcoming titles and events
please join our mailing list by completing the form on the website.
You can also follow Flapjack Press on Twitter @FlapjackPress
or find us on Facebook.

Flapjack Press: exploring the synergy between performance and the page.